love
and peace
through affirmation

love
and peace
through affirmation

by carole a. daxter

H J Kramer Inc
Tiburon, California

H J Kramer Inc
P.O. Box 1082
Tiburon, CA 94920

Library of Congress Cataloging-in-Publication Data

Daxter, Carole.
  Love and peace through affirmation / by Carole Daxter.
    p.   cm.
  ISBN 0-915811-18-9 : $7.95
  1. Conduct of life. 2. Success. 3. Meditations. I. Title.
BJ1581.2.D39   1989
291.4'3—dc20   89-83665
                                                          CIP

Editor: Nancy Carleton
Cover Art: Pat Powers
Cover Design: Spectra Media
Type by: Classic Typography
Book Production: Schuettge and Carleton

Manufactured in the United States of America

10   9   8   7   6   5   4   3   2   1

dedication

*With the love of the Universe, I dedicate
and share with you thoughts and words that
will bring love, peace, and harmony.*

In time of need, run your fingers through the book
and ask, "What is the affirmation for me today?"
Where your finger stops is your answer.

TO OUR READERS

The books we publish are our contribution to an emerging world based on cooperation rather than on competition, on affirmation of the human spirit rather than on self-doubt, and on the certainty that all humanity is connected. Our goal is to touch as many lives as possible with a message of hope for a better world.

Hal and Linda Kramer, Publishers

ACKNOWLEDGMENTS:

I thank the Universe for guiding all the right people into my life who have influenced me and helped me to grow.

I thank my husband, Brian, for his continued support; without him, this book might never have been created.

I thank my family and friends. Just by being in my life, they have contributed to my growth and understanding.

I thank the following authors: Catherine Ponder, Colin P. Sisson, U.S. Anderson, Louise L. Hay, Robert A. Monroe, and Kahlil Gibran. In reading their material, I have expanded my knowledge and this has enabled me to help others.

I thank my daughter, Tracy Kenworthy, and her partner, Geoffrey Bickford, for being in tune and presenting graphics harmonious with the message to the heart.

Special thanks to Wilma John, who partook in the tedious task of proofreading and editing.

TABLE OF CONTENTS

FOREWORD

My life was in a mess: two broken marriages, the death of a child, and no direction. I contemplated suicide; my life didn't seem worth living. A friend told me about thinking positive! I thought I *was* positive, but little did I realize how negative I really was!

Then I changed. How? By affirming beautiful positive thoughts and words to myself each day. Sure, there were times when the old emotions came flooding in, but I plodded on and kept up the affirmations. I realized that it was I, and only I, who was responsible for my life. That it was I who had to do something about it. Being basically a lazy person, I found that there were many times I gave up, only to begin again. I realized that when I was affirming beautiful, loving, positive thoughts and words, I felt good about myself and all around me.

This has led me to a more rewarding life, newfound confidence, and a feeling of security and peace. Through my channeling, my clairvoyance, and the personal development workshops I run, I have shared affirmations with others. I firmly believe this has helped me. The feedback from these people has always been very positive.

Now I have been prompted to write this book and share with you the harmony, peace, prosperity, and love that affirmations have brought into my life, in the knowledge that you, too, can experience them. The beautiful part about all of this is it doesn't matter what age we are; it is up to us to create changes for ourselves. Affirmations can help us achieve this.

There is really nothing new in what I am presenting here, just my viewpoint. The challenge I make to you is: Don't believe what I say—try it and see what happens!

You may ask, "What will happen if I decide to do this?" You will learn to like yourself more, which will lead to liking others more. You will learn to feel good in your workplace. You will learn to feel great about your finances. You will learn to feel wonderful on this planet. You will learn to be happy. You will learn—love!

WHAT ARE AFFIRMATIONS?

An affirmation is merely a group of words put together to make a sentence. That sentence is the affirmation. It expresses what we want from life. Being explicit is crucial. Many people have recommended short, snappy affirmations, and that's all right, provided we know what the affirmation means. I prefer to be precise.

For instance, "I am prosperity" is a fantastic affirmation, but what does it mean? Does it mean an abundance in everything? Does it mean an abundance in just one area? Prosperity means different things to different people. I found at the beginning that I needed to affirm very precisely what I wanted to prosper in. I affirmed, "I prosper in love. I prosper in good health. I prosper in financial areas." Finally, I could say, "I am prosperity," and *know that I am.*

I see life as a game of semantics, a game of words. If we care to be honest with ourselves, that is really all life is. As we look at our daily lives, what are we really doing? We are following a pattern! First comes the thought, which is then verbalized. Then we find this thought becoming reality, because we have acted upon it. *This pattern applies to both negative and positive thoughts. This process is happening every moment of our lives, even though we may not recognize it as such.* Our desires, whether negative or positive, are brought about with this pattern of thinking and affirming.

The strongest force comes from the emotions we attach to affirmations. Remember feeling really frightened about something—and then it happened? Of course it did, because we focused our thoughts on it, coupled with the emotion of fear, and we created it. That's the negative side. The positive side works in the same way, with one slight difference: No emotions need be attached to the thought.

I do recommend, however, that any positive affirmation, whether it is thought silently or said out loud, should be felt, believed, and then released without attaching any emotion to that affirmation. In this way, the process is set into motion more quickly.

HOW DO AFFIRMATIONS WORK?

We are all created from the same source—pure love. That powerful unconditional love is within us all, and it vibrates on a frequency that we have buried and are not always able to recognize. Perhaps we even think that we don't possess it. But we do—each and every one of us—we all have this same power—pure love. So to trigger this beautiful power within us, we need to relearn or reprogram ourselves with good, positive, loving, peaceful thoughts and words.

These words will filter through to the truth and love within and will allow us to become that power totally. Through this process, our pattern of thinking becomes our reality, and it feels good. It is good!

HOW DO WE
USE AFFIRMATIONS?

First, we decide on the area in which we wish to change. Let's make it easy for ourselves and start with something simple and basic. For instance, "I am happy to change." Think it, say it out loud, write it down. To start off with, write it at least fifty times. If that feels too much, write it as many times as feels comfortable. The key is to allow ourselves to feel good and feel comfortable about what we wish to make true for ourselves.

Then keep thinking, saying, or writing the affirmation over and over on a daily basis. Do not let impatience creep in (for it does at the beginning), just keep affirming. This process of repetition prepares us for the next stage—namely, that *we believe it!* There are no time limits on how long we concentrate on one affirmation. I find that if I have a "low energy" day I use affirmations I started years ago—they are always with me.

I write my affirmations on cards and place them on my mirror, so I can see them first thing in the morning. I put them on my bedside table, and read them before falling asleep at night. I put them in my car, so I can affirm as I drive.

Saying the affirmations out loud is beneficial, for when we speak our body vibrates physically. In this way, we speak it, we hear it, and the impact is powerful. Record affirmations on tape over and over and play the tape back while you rest or sleep.

SAY THE WORDS. FEEL THE WORDS. BELIEVE THE WORDS. THEN KNOW THE AFFIRMATION IS YOU.

Please be gentle with yourself. I know I experienced impatience, frustration, and anger many times, but I kept plodding on, for the key is never giving up. The result of using affirmations in a repetitive way is simple. First you *think* about it, then you *believe* it, and then you *know* it is true for you.

I wish you well on your pathway of using affirmations to obtain a healthier, happier, more fulfilling life.

To know which particular affirmation in this book is right for you at any time, just hold the book and ask the question, "What affirmation is appropriate for me today?" Open where your finger falls and, presto, you have it! You can use this affirmation just for the day or continue with it for some time.

The affirmations presented here are a guide. When you become successful in using them, you'll be able to create your own. Remember though, affirmations must always be in the present tense, for it is only *now* that we are dealing with. It may not be evident right at this moment, but the *now* of realization is not far off.

I THINK, I BELIEVE, I KNOW.

good morning universe

I happily greet this day with excitement,
for I am happy to be alive. I give thanks, for
today is complete and unfolds to me
miraculous, wondrous things. This day is
perfect for me.

I think
I am happy to
bring beautiful
changes to me now.

I believe
I am happy to
bring beautiful
changes to me now.

I know
I am happy to
bring beautiful
changes to me now.

I am change.

change

In the past I experienced difficulty when I tried to bring changes into my life. I recognize now that it is very simple to bring about beautiful changes in my life. I only need to choose a happy life, then change my limiting thoughts to limitless ones. I think I can. I believe I can. I know I can, for the guiding force within me knows only peace and harmony and I am guided to the truth within.

I am change.

I think
I have confidence in
me and all I do.

I believe
I have confidence in
me and all I do.

I know
I have confidence in
me and all I do.

I am confidence.

confidence

My fear of failure often prevented me from learning new things. A feeling of panic surged within me, preventing me from even trying. I recognize that in trying I have succeeded. In this knowledge, I have confidence in myself and I know it is O.K to do new things in a way that is comfortable for me.

I am confidence.

I think
I communicate with
ease.

I believe
I communicate with
ease.

I know
I communicate with
ease.

I am
communication.

communication

There have been times when I have had difficulty in saying what I really wanted to say, for fear that I would appear silly. As time passes I recognize that it is safe for me to verbalize my thoughts and feelings, for they are a part of me. As I understand myself and others, I believe I can communicate equally with all I meet. I have no fear of ridicule, because I will know that with the power within I communicate easily and lovingly.

I am communication.

I think
I am responsible
for my life .

I believe
I am responsible
for my life .

I know
I am responsible
for my life .

I am responsibility .

responsibility

In the past I felt the weight of responsibility and made it a burden for myself. Now I look and see that this was a learning experience. I believe that I can move through life with ease, for my ability to respond to all events is getting better every day in every way. I know that the power within allows me the strength and courage to accept my responsibilities with love.

I am responsibility.

I think
I express my life
easily and lovingly.

I believe
I express my life
easily and lovingly.

I know
I express my life
easily and lovingly.

I am life.

In the past I quickly blamed everything around me when my life seemed to be traumatic. The mirrors in my life showed that the stress, trauma, and chaos was of my own doing. In the expansion of my knowledge, I believe that to change my life I can now choose to open myself to accept new, wonderful things. My heart sings with joy, for I now express life with love, peace, and harmony. Life is good for me.

I am life.

I think
I am honest with
me and I am an
expression of that
honesty.

I believe
I am honest with
me and I am an
expression of that
honesty.

I know
I am honest with
me and I am an
expression of that
honesty.

I am honesty.

All my life I have been governed by rules and regulations on what is honest and what is not. That is O.K. I was afraid to be honest with myself and recognize emotions there. I now understand that honesty is being truthful with the power within. This honesty gives understanding and strength, which is valuable knowledge for me.

I am honesty.

I think
I am a loving,
forgiving person.

I believe
I am a loving,
forgiving person.

I know
I am a loving,
forgiving person.

I am forgiveness.

forgiveness

My past experiences have gone, but why do I remember with pain? I cannot change my past, but I can change how I feel about it right now. "To err is human, to forgive divine." I believe I release all emotions attached to memories. I forgive and release all past events and people. I release them to their highest good, as I am released to mine. I now know that the events of my past were there to help me grow and, with this knowledge, I now let go and become free.

I am forgiveness.

I think
it is easy to trust
everything because
I have trust in me.

I believe
it is easy to trust
everything because
I have trust in me.

I know
it is easy to trust
everything because
I have trust in me.

I am trust.

trust

When I was born into this life, I had
complete trust in all things around me.
Somehow, somewhere, as I grew older, I lost
that trust. 'Being aware of this, I would now
like to trust myself and the universe again. I
believe that by regaining trust I will be
relieved of all restrictions and limitations. I
will then know that if I trust in myself and
the universe I will readily attract beautiful
things to me easily.

I am trust.

I think
I am free to be me .

I believe
I am free to be me .

I know
I am free to be me .

I am me .

me

All my life I tried to copy qualities I saw in others which I didn't think I possessed. I always wished I was someone else and not me. As I understood that people only reflected me, I was overjoyed to find those qualities were, in fact, in me. I happily stroll through life now, in the knowledge that there is no one else exactly like me. I am free because I am me and I am beautiful.

I am me.

I think
I am a friend to
myself and others.

I believe
I am a friend to
myself and others.

I know
I am a friend to
myself and others.

I am friendship.

As I walk the corridor of my life, I see mirrors which reflect not only me, but my friends. In these mirrors the image reflected is not always to my liking, but that is O.K, for I can work on that. I know it is me, and I am learning to grow; in my growth, the friendship I develop with myself will be the only friendship I require. In becoming a friend to myself, I know that all the friends of the universe will be with me.

I am friendship.

I think
I am a caring,
sharing person.

I believe
I am a caring,
sharing person.

I know
I am a caring,
sharing person.

I am sharing.

sharing

When I was young I was told to share,
but I couldn't understand why, for I believed
things were mine. As I unravel what is truth
for me, I now understand that nothing is
mine. The universe supplies all things for me
to use and share with others in a wonderful,
loving way. By sharing myself in a caring
way, I know I am sharing the power within,
for we are one.

I am sharing.

I think
I give freely and
unconditionally.

I believe
I give freely and
unconditionally.

I know
I give freely and
unconditionally.

I am giving.

giving

In the past giving was pleasing, yet I put conditions on the gift. In looking, I saw that I gave to seek approval and with expectations of something in return. I now believe my heart is filled with love and I can give unconditionally anything I desire. I know that the power within is both the giver and the gift. By giving lovingly, I am giving freely and everything returns to me tenfold in the same way — freely.

I am giving.

I think
I accept myself and
all things totally.

I believe
I accept myself and
all things totally.

I know
I accept myself and
all things totally.

I am acceptance.

acceptance

Throughout my life I have had difficulty accepting, because I had placed conditions on acceptance. As I grow to understand myself, I believe I am now able to open myself happily to accept new, wonderful events and people into my life. As I grow, and as I accept all things unconditionally and look upon them as my teachers, my knowledge will expand for my divine good. In acceptance, I see all things clearly, as good and beautiful.

I am acceptance.

I think
I relax and rest
easily.

I believe
I relax and rest
easily.

I know
I relax and rest
easily.

I am restfulness.

restfulness

I have often felt my body twitch and ache and have had many a sleepless night. My mind dwelt on things of the day and worried about what might happen next. When I relax, I find I see things more clearly and my body rests. The deep breath of the universe fills me with restfulness and I am at ease.

I am restfulness.

I think
I have all the
strength I require.

I believe
I have all the
strength I require.

I know
I have all the
strength I require.

I am strength.

Strength is not assertive or aggressive.
Strength comes from the pure essence of love.
This strength gives me the ability to respond
to every event in my life in a gentle, caring,
loving way. The strength I receive is from the
universe, and it allows me to have all the
support I require so that I will move through
life with ease.

I am strength.

I think
I express life gently
with love .

I believe
I express life gently
with love .

I know
I express life gently
with love .

I am gentleness .

gentleness

I have often thought, "He is gentle, he must be weak." I can now see there is great strength in gentleness, for it reflects much understanding, caring, and peace. Gentleness is a true gift of the universe, and there is a great power there, for it comes only from love.

I am gentleness.

I think
I receive gracefully.

I believe
I receive gracefully.

I know
I receive gracefully.

I am receiving.

receiving

I had always been taught "It is better to give than to receive." I have always felt uncomfortable when receiving, but I know the pleasure I feel when I give. So why should I take that away from anybody? I see now that to receive gracefully is a gift in itself. As I grow to like myself, I see that I am worthy of receiving.

I am receiving.

*I think
I am healthy in
mind, body, and
affairs.*

*I believe
I am healthy in
mind, body, and
affairs.*

*I know
I am healthy in
mind, body, and
affairs.*

I am healthy.

health

Along the way there have been many times that I have experienced ill health or disease. As I search within, I find I was created from pure love, and in pure love there can be no ill health. I believe I can change my outlook in ways that are comfortable to me. I now know that it is my divine right to experience a beautiful, happy, healthy existence — and I do.

I am healthy.

I think
I see joy in
everything.

I believe
I see joy in
everything.

I know
I see joy in
everything.

I am joy.

joy

I had always looked to others to bring joy
into my life. I know it is the way I see
things that interprets them as either
miserable or joyful. I now choose to see all
things in my life with joy. I joyfully create
good health, love, and contentment. I am
happy to be me, and I am filled with joy.

I am joy.

I think
I have an endless
supply of energy to
use.

I believe
I have an endless
supply of energy to
use.

I know
I have an endless
supply of energy to
use.

I am energy.

energy

There are times when I have felt low on
energy. These have usually turned into
depressing times, for I have allowed my
thoughts to run riot. I try all things to give me
a boost: good diet, exercise, and fun things to
do, but still the energy fades. My negative
beliefs make me that way. I now see that all
the pure energy of the universe is for me to use
at all times. I call on the pure energy of the
universe to flow through me now to help me do
the things I want to do.

I am energy.

*I think
my mind, my
body, and my affairs
are in divine order.*

*I believe
my mind, my
body, and my affairs
are in divine order.*

*I know
my mind, my
body, and my affairs
are in divine order.*

I am order.

order

Many times I have wept because I felt life had dealt me a raw blow, and I experienced disorder. I sought advice from others on what to do. However, the final choice was up to me. Do I want order in my life? Yes, please! I receive order and enlightenment in my life, for it is my divine right. I am willing to change my attitude to bring divine order into my life.

I am order.

I think
I respect myself
and others.

I believe
I respect myself
and others.

I know
I respect myself
and others.

I am respect.

My mirror images are all around me, and when I haven't respected them I recognized it was definitely something in me. I felt unworthy of respect. We are all created equally, and I learn easily to respect myself and others. I am 100 percent worthy of all things at all times.

I am respect.

I think
I have the power to
control my life.

I believe
I have the power to
control my life.

I know
I have the power to
control my life.

I am power.

power

Passing through the crossroads of life, I
have often given power to others by allowing
their remarks to cut deep into my heart. The
cutting remarks only had power because I
related them to self. Had I listened only to
their words and placed no emotional
attachments to them, I would have
understood they were telling me something of
themselves. I now believe and understand
that the power within me is truth, wisdom,
and harmony.

I am power.

good day
universe

I give thanks to the Universe for this day. I
see the magic, the wonder, and the
enlightenment in each moment as it unfolds
for me. I feel wonderful today! Today is
perfect for me.

I think
I praise myself and
all around me. I
see good in
everything.

I believe
I praise myself and
all around me. I
see good in
everything.

I know
I praise myself and
all around me. I
see good in
everything.

I am praise.

praise

How often have I been quick to criticize and see the bad in all. That is all I recognized. Now I praise everyone and every situation in my life, for I know I see good there. What I focus on, I bring into my life. I now only desire all that is good for me and others. I praise and give thanks as the universe unfolds everything perfectly for me now.

I am praise.

I think
I understand all
things perfectly.

I believe
I understand all
things perfectly.

I know
I understand all
things perfectly.

I am
understanding.

understanding

How often have I said, "But you don't understand . . ." All my life I sought love and understanding from others and not myself. I believe that as I expand my knowledge and come to a better understanding of the universe, I can change my world. A ray of sunshine fills my being as the power within gives me understanding of all things.

I am understanding.

I think
I give thanks for
my life.

I believe
I give thanks for
my life.

I know
I give thanks for
my life.

I am gratitude.

gratitude

On reflection, I see many moments in my past that I did not give thanks for. It is only now that I see how much I can be grateful for. I am eternally grateful for my pathway, for I have learned many things. I see now that I was always at the right place, at the right time, every moment of my life. I believe that to show gratitude, thanks, and even praise for all things in my life will make it more rewarding and fulfilling. My heart sings gratefully.

I am gratitude.

I think
I bring happiness
to myself and
others.

I believe
I bring happiness
to myself and
others.

I know
I bring happiness
to myself and
others.

I am happiness.

happiness

I was always taught to try and make others happy. That is true. I now see that in order to bring this about I must first begin with myself. As I look within, I see the universal happiness there. I now know that my happiness is contagious and will attract greater happiness. I know that by being happy in what I do my universe will be happy too.

I am happiness.

I think
I happily live life
spontaneously .

I believe
I happily live life
spontaneously .

I know
I happily live life
spontaneously .

I am spontaneity.

spontaneity

The child within me loved to be
impulsive and live life spontaneously. This
was lost after restrictions, scorn, and
disapproval were imposed on me. I see I
imposed restrictions on me. I now believe
that it is really OK to express myself and my
life spontaneously. I know that the actions are
brought to me by loving energy, and to be
spontaneous simply means to allow the child
within to be free.

I am spontaneity.

I think
I am unlimited
inspiration, and I
act accordingly.

I believe
I am unlimited
inspiration, and I
act accordingly.

I know
I am unlimited
inspiration, and I
act accordingly.

I am inspiration.

inspiration

Inspiration comes and goes. It is what I do with it that counts. For inspiration is not for a few, but for all. Inspiration can give me the key to enlightenment and growth. I believe my inspiration is from the power within, and I know there are no limitations there. As I gaze at the beauty around me, I know that the creator was inspired by love, and I am that loving inspiration.

I am inspiration.

I think
I am listening and
learning.

I believe
I am listening and
learning.

I know
I am listening and
learning.

I am listening.

listening

All too often I have closed my ears and not heard all that was said. This led me to anger, frustration, and fear. Now I recognize that when I listen openly I hear words that are helpful to me. I learn with every word that is spoken. I hear clearly the voice of the universe as it always guides me to my highest good.

I am listening.

*I think
I can image all
things beautiful for
me and others.*

*I believe
I can image all
things beautiful for
me and others.*

*I know
I can image all
things beautiful for
me and others.*

I am imagination.

imagination

There have been many times in my
life when I have felt scolded for using
my imagination. As I learn to expand
my knowledge and learn what is truth for me,
I believe that to imagine is good. What
I imagine as divine good for me and others
will come to pass, for coupled with belief,
my imagining can bring me love, peace,
harmony, good health, and success.
In imagining, I see with the eyes of the
power within and see all things clearly.

I am imagination.

I think
I have laughter in
my life.

I believe
I have laughter in
my life.

I know
I have laughter in
my life.

I am laughter.

laughter

I cast my mind back to my childhood days and see myself with joy and laughter in my heart. It was the true wisdom of the child that brought laugher to me and others. I was able to accept all things into my life with glee and happiness. Now I believe and know the same child within me can laugh, be joyous, and be free, for the power within laughs with me.

I am laughter.

I think
I create my life
lovingly.

I believe
I create my life
lovingly.

I know
I create my life
lovingly.

I am creativity.

There have been times when the envy of
others' creativity has crept in. As I grow and
expand my knowledge, I believe
that it is my choice to be creative. I am the
creator of my world with every thought and
word I express. I now choose to create love
and happiness in every thought and word for
myself and others.

I am creativity.

I think
I prosper in all
things.

I believe
I prosper in all
things.

I know
I prosper in all
things.

I am prosperity.

prosperity

I have pondered many times, "Why am I poor?" I see others prosperous. This comparison limits me, as I recognize only their abundance and not my own. I thought I was lacking. I now believe to prosper simply means to do things in a way that will bring me pleasure. Prosperity is for all, not just a few. I prosper in love. I prosper in health. I prosper in joy. Prosperity is only a state of mind, and I am in that state of mind right now.

I am prosperity.

I think
I achieve all things
successfully.

I believe
I achieve all things
successfully.

I know
I achieve all things
successfully.

I am success.

SUCCESS

There have been times when my attitude
was unbecoming. I wilfully reacted to people
and events with anger and resentment. The
only one hurt was I. I recognize I can
achieve more by being calm. I now know by
changing my attitude to all things around me
I find success in everything I do.

I am success.

I think
I am rich in love
and happiness.

I believe
I am rich in love
and happiness.

I know
I am rich in love
and happiness.

I am rich.

rich

I had been conditioned to believe that rich
simply meant lots of money. When I probe
the corners of my mind, I see that the truth
within says this is not so. For to be rich is
simply to lead my life to the fullest and to be
rich in love. I believe
I am rich, for the power within has shown me
my riches. In releasing all my wants and
needs, I can see that all is provided. I bathe in
the rich gold substance of the universe because
I deserve it.

I am rich.

I think
I have unshakable
faith in the power
within.

I believe
I have unshakable
faith in the power
within.

I know
I have unshakable
faith in the power
within.

I am faith.

*The expression of my life unfolds
lovingly as I learn and understand that faith
overcomes all fears. With faith, I believe
the universe unfolds for me all that is perfect
for my divine good. In faith, I move in an
upward, progressive movement of life, and I
know
every situation is perfect for me.*

I am faith.

I think
I listen to and
follow all intuitive
leads.

I believe
I listen to and
follow all intuitive
leads.

I know
I listen to and
follow all intuitive
leads.

I am intuition.

intuition

Travelling along life's path I have unravelled many mysteries that have now become knowledge and truth. In my search I have found that the only limitations I had were placed there by me. I now know that to have intuition is really only being finely tuned and aware of Self. I also know that the power within is pure love, and it is this loving guidance that is given. My choice is to listen and follow that intuition, knowing and trusting that it will lead me to a beautiful, wondrous life.

I am intuition.

*I think
I am loving to
myself and I
express divine love
fully.*

*I believe
I am loving to
myself and I
express divine love
fully.*

*I know
I am loving to
myself and I
express divine love
fully.*

I am love.

love

It seems I hurt most when I felt that no one loved me. Here I go again — looking to others to fulfill my needs. I was looking to the outside, when all the time the love I was seeking was within me. The love within me is giving, caring, and unconditional. The love within is the pure essence of life, and I am that pure essence of love.

I am love.

I think
I make decisions
wisely and quickly.

I believe
I make decisions
wisely and quickly.

I know
I make decisions
wisely and quickly.

I am wisdom.

wisdom

In my youth I would change my mind
frequently, for I thought I had decided quickly
and unwisely. I would often wait and see
what others might do. I now recognize that I
was unsure of myself and not prepared to take
risks. As my understanding grows, I know
that I have a super wisdom of truth within
me. I know I make decisions wisely, for I am
that wisdom.

I am wisdom.

I think
I have peace in my
life.

I believe
I have peace in my
life.

I know
I have peace in my
life.

I am peace.

peace

With peace in my life, I find a stillness, a place of quiet. It is the center of my being. This peace is a beautiful place of knowing that the universe will unfold to me all knowledge, understanding, and truth for me. Peace brings no comparisons, simply being— being one with the divine source.

I am peace.

I think
I feel tranquility in
all things.

I believe
I feel tranquility in
all things.

I know
I feel tranquility in
all things.

I am tranquility.

I wish to bring tranquility into my life. I
do this by not having expectations of myself
and others. I am slow to anger, for I do not
force my will onto others. Instead, loving,
caring thoughts and words will express my
tranquility, for I come from a tranquil place.
I know that tranquility is divine love.

I am tranquility.

I think
I am free of all
limitations.

I believe
I am free of all
limitations.

I know
I am free of all
limitations.

I am freedom.

freedom

I often punished myself with loads of guilt for I felt I hadn't lived up to others' expectations, or my own. There is no stronger critic of me than myself. Happily, I see I am free from guilt because, in not having expectations, I now know I will never be disappointed. I am free to express my life in a way that is easy for me.

I am freedom.

I think
I am harmonious
in mind, body, and
spirit.

I believe
I am harmonious
in mind, body, and
spirit.

I know
I am harmonious
in mind, body, and
spirit.

I am harmony.

harmony

Like the well-rehearsed orchestra, I will
be happy to learn with each new experience.
I will learn to the best of my ability and that is
O.K, for I am unique. I will be happy to
grow and bring harmony to mind, body, and
spirit. I believe there is harmony within me,
within all my relationships, and all around
me. In harmony, I feel complete. I have found
life rewarding, for I am in harmony.

I am harmony.

I think
I release all
judgments, and I
am balanced.

I believe
I release all
judgments, and I
am balanced.

I know
I release all
judgments, and I
am balanced.

I am balance.

balance

With all the learned negativity I have
absorbed on the way, I have become
judgmental. This has led me to criticize
others and myself. I criticize and I judge
because I compare how I think life should be
with what I actually see. I know that to
achieve perfect balance all I need to do is see
that the universe around me is perfect. It is
only my perception and comparisons that
make it otherwise. The power within me only
recognizes perfect harmony and balance.

I am balance.

I think
I live totally in the
now; it is the only
moment with me.

I believe
I live totally in the
now; it is the only
moment with me.

I know
I live totally in the
now; it is the only
moment with me.

I am now.

All my life I have concerned myself with
the "What ifs," the "If onlys" and the
"Tomorrows." I lived for either yesterday or
tomorrow and forgot about now. This very
moment is the only time that matters and
I refuse to wait until tomorrow, for it is now
that I am in paradise. I believe that when
I focus on now it is the beginning of a new
happy life for me. The power within knows
no time, so to exist in that power I live only in
the now.

I am now.

good evening universe

I give thanks for this beautiful day.
I happily rest in the knowledge that what I
experienced today was perfect for me in every
way. I will awake in the morning with love,
peace, and joy.

I give thanks for this special day. I create loving thoughts and words for myself and others today. I am happy. I am at peace.

[Suggested affirmations to use for this day.
Add your desired affirmation.]

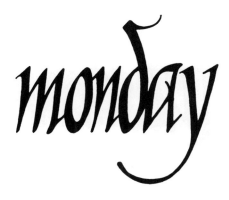

*I give thanks for this perfect, wondrous
day. I smile happily as I greet this day.
I smile happily at all I meet. I work efficiently
and with joy.*

[Suggested affirmations to use for this day.
Add your desired affirmation.]

I give thanks for this magical day. This day unfolds happy surprises, and I accept gracefully.

[Suggested affirmations to use for this day.
Add your desired affirmation.]

Wednesday

Thanks for today. I find today a day of communication, and I communicate easily and happily.

[Suggested affirmations to use for this day. Add your desired affirmation.]

*I am thankful for this day. Today
I praise all I meet, and I see the good in
everything today.*

[Suggested affirmations to use for this day.
Add your desired affirmation.]

Love, love, love. I lovingly say
thank you for today. The love I have within
me touches everyone I meet.

[Suggested affirmations to use for this day.
Add your desired affirmation.]

I give thanks for the boundless supply of energy I have within me. I am grateful for today.

[Suggested affirmations to use for this day.
Add your desired affirmation.]

CONCLUSION

I realized while in the process of putting this book together that we can all gain so much faith and strength simply by reading the affirmations, saying them over and over again until our lives feel good all the time. Every day, in every way, we are getting better and better.

As thoughts and words are powerful, so powerful that with each one we create our lives, I now choose to exercise care with my thoughts and words simply because I wish to create a loving world for myself and others around me.

Surely, if we wish to have a happy, peaceful world, we need to start with ourselves.

I know you will find the same happy, peaceful environment and will benefit greatly from using all positive affirmations.

As you read this book and apply the affirmations daily, I congratulate you, for you have now begun changing yourself and your world.

Yours in Love and Peace,

Carole Daxter

ABOUT THE AUTHOR

Carole is a Western Australian born and based clairvoyant, channeler, and personal development practitioner. A wife and mother of four, Carole experienced many traumatic events in her life that brought her to a crossroad—suicide or change?

Carole chose the latter and explored the reasons her life had become so unhappy. In her search for something better, studying metaphysics opened a happy, healthy new pathway.

Carole believes thoughts and spoken words are the most powerful tools at our fingertips. She has used affirmations daily in her growth work. Now, Carole shares, guides, and supports those who attend her courses.

In addition to offering personal development and healing courses, Carole and her husband Brian serve as Reiki therapists, spiritual counselors, and friends to all they meet.

You can write to Carole Daxter at
P.O. Box 661
Kalamunda 6076
Western Australia

BOOKS THAT TRANSFORM LIVES
FROM H J KRAMER INC

ORIN BOOKS
by
Sanaya Roman
The Earth Life Series is a course in learning to live with joy, sense energy, and grow spiritually.

LIVING WITH JOY, BOOK I
"I like this book because it describes the way I feel about so many things."—Virginia Satir

PERSONAL POWER THROUGH AWARENESS: A GUIDEBOOK FOR SENSITIVE PEOPLE, BOOK II
"Every sentence contains a pearl . . ."—Lilias Folan

SPIRITUAL GROWTH: BEING YOUR HIGHER SELF, BOOK III
Orin teaches how to reach upward to align with the higher energies of the universe, look inward to expand awareness, and move outward in world service.

JOY IN A WOOLLY COAT: GRIEF SUPPORT FOR PET LOSS
by
Julie Adams Church
JOY IN A WOOLLY COAT is about living with, loving, and letting go of treasured animal friends.

EAT FOR HEALTH: A DO-IT-YOURSELF NUTRITION GUIDE FOR SOLVING COMMON MEDICAL PROBLEMS
by
William Manahan, M.D.
"Essential reading and an outstanding selection."
—Library Journal

YOU THE HEALER: THE WORLD-FAMOUS SILVA METHOD ON HOW TO HEAL YOURSELF AND OTHERS
by
José Silva and Robert B. Stone
YOU THE HEALER is the complete course in the Silva Method healing techniques presented in a do-it-yourself forty-day format.

SEEDS OF LIGHT
by
Peter Rengel
Poetry on varied subjects to help align you with your higher self

BOOKS THAT TRANSFORM LIVES
FROM H J KRAMER INC

WAY OF THE PEACEFUL WARRIOR
by
Dan Millman
Available in book and audio cassette format.
A tale of spiritual adventure . . . a worldwide bestseller!

An Orin/DaBen Book
OPENING TO CHANNEL:
HOW TO CONNECT WITH YOUR GUIDE
by
Sanaya Roman and Duane Packer, Ph.D.
This breakthrough book is the first
step-by-step guide to the art of channeling.

TALKING WITH NATURE
by
Michael J. Roads
A guidebook to help you align with the energies
of the plant and animal kingdoms.

An Orin/DaBen Book
CREATING MONEY
by
Sanaya Roman and Duane Packer, Ph.D.
"To be considered required reading
for those who aspire to financial well-being."
—Body Mind Spirit

WHAT IS YOUR PSI-Q?
by
Petey Stevens
America's leading psychic teacher introduces
the reader to his or her psychic potential.

SINGING MAN
by
Neil Anderson
"One of the finest allegories of our time . . . a story
of everyman in transition."—Jean Houston

BIOCIRCUITS: AMAZING NEW TOOLS
FOR ENERGY HEALTH
by
Leslie Patten with Terry Patten
"A well-written eye-opener on the most exciting field
in science today—the study of the body's electrical and
quasi-electrical energy."—Michael Hutchison